# the Promise

You can have what you *really* want.

## Mark Whitwell

**urban family**

Printed in the United States of America
First Printing, 2015
ISBN 978-0692553879

*Published by:*
Urban Family Foundation
P.O. Box 5875, Berkeley, CA
United States 94705
urbanfamily.org

*Design and Typesetting by:*
Brian James Kroeker / burningheartstudio.net
*Yoga Photos by:* Debra Stapleton
*Yoga Model:* Brian James Kroeker

*Information:* heartofyoga.org
Download the iPromise app on iTunes and Google Play

## THE RED THREAD

An ancient Chinese myth speaks of an invisible
red thread which connects those who are destined to
meet, regardless of time, place, or circumstances,
or those who are otherwise meant to help each other
in some way. It's said that the thread may stretch or
tangle but will never break.

As you read this book, I invite you to use a red thread
as a placeholder, and when you are ready to make
The Promise and practice for 40 days, wear it on your
wrist as a symbol of your connection.

Throughout the book you'll see the red thread marking
the exercises of The Promise Practice. Take a few
minutes to try each exercise as they appear, by the end
of the book you'll have learned the complete practice.

"YOGA IS YOUR DIRECT EMBRACE OF THE POWER OF THIS COSMOS PRESENTLY ARISING...

...AS PURE
INTELLIGENCE,
NURTURING
AND
THE UTTER
BEAUTY OF LIFE
THAT IS YOU."

## ACKNOWLEDGMENT

"I release *The Promise* with recognition and gratitude for the Great Tradition in its entirety, wherever it has appeared throughout time, threaded through all geographies and cultures.

I give thanks to all who have added their hearts to the wisdom of humanity, including in our own time U.G. Krishnamurti and T. Krishnamacharya, and to all of you who carry it forward with clarity to all people and all cultures of modern times.

Humanity has created dark days for ourselves at the time of writing this book. It may not be what we want or asked for, but it's what we've been given. It's the shift we're on. We have been chosen to be here at this time alongside the frightened, the under-informed and the fundamentalism of East and West. Let us work ceaselessly in the wound of love to inform the citizenry that everything is as it should be. EveryOne *is* connected and *is* in the embrace of that which *is* great. The power of this cosmos *is* arising as everyOne, as pure intelligence, perfect nurturing and the beauty that *is you*. Enjoy this fact and pass it on even in the midst of mass fear and climate chaos. Let's each make our stand and use our vast human collaboration, intelligence, technologies and love that *is* surging through us; to cooperate with our Mother Nature.

I give thanks to all my friends who helped birth The Promise, and to Emmanuel Briand, Brian Kroeker, Stephanie Majcher and Kathy Wyre for your brilliance."

*Mark Whitwell*
*Berkeley, California, December 2015*

# PREFACE

W hy have I titled this book *The Promise: You can have what you really want*? It is simply true that anyone who wants to can practice advanced yoga. Yoga is not a matter of difficult attainments toward a future result. Yoga is your direct participation in the nurturing power of this cosmos that is presently arising as the pure intelligence, function and the beauty of life that is you. No matter your age or health or cultural background, you can do this. By participating in the union of your inhalation and exhalation using simple body movements to empower your breath, your strength and receptivity will increase. The male and female power of your own life will be activated within you and with your intimate partner. If you enhance the breath, all other critical functions of your health will improve.

This yoga is a catalyst that brings forth all your skills and life potentials. It creates intimacy with life in every way including a sublime love connection with your special other. It activates and sustains love in ways that will astound you. I promise you this!

"IF YOU HAVE THE COURAGE
TO TOUCH LIFE FOR THE FIRST TIME,
YOU WON'T KNOW WHAT HIT YOU."
U.G. KRISHNAMURTI

# INTRODUCTION

You can have what you *really* want. Really. And that is my promise to you. The Promise Practice will give you sublime connection to life in new and interesting ways that the usual lifestyle does not touch. And it is easy. You will feel an intimacy with life in every way including your potential to love and be loved with strength and receptivity. This I promise.

The unprecedented and rapid change of the last two centuries has opened the world — and led us to a place where we need some help, perhaps some ancient wisdom, to feel that we belong in our own reality. Our lives are less isolated yet more disconnected than ever. It is the worst and the best of times because real help is being communicated worldwide as we reach out amidst dreadful uncertainties. There are more illusions and more pain than ever in our way. Having seen through the myth of the materialistic dream, the investigation of other ways of looking at the world has become an appealing option. In the process, so-called "enlightenment" has been presented as a convincing antidote to the dissatisfaction of lives subjected to society's preoccupation with productivity and acquisition. The popular fascination with yoga, meditation and other spiritual practices indicates a genuine desire for personal development and victory over life difficulties. Yet the mass marketing of inner peace is not always benign and can be another form of consumerism in a marketplace of shoddy spiritual goods. This seduction of enlightenment creates a sense of emptiness and hunger for fulfillment no less illusive as any other addiction. Often in this search to find a solution to the ills of modern life, we get caught in a compulsive cycle not dissimilar to the very thing from which we were trying to break free. We are desperate consumers either waiting for a miracle savior to return or waiting for enlightenment to arrive. But have we learned to embrace our own wonder?

The truth is that most of us aren't actually looking to transcend life, but to fully enjoy the life we have. And here's the rub: the merchandising of inner peace has started yet another war raging within and without. The goals of the great wisdom teachings have been presented as impossible ideals for those of us leading "normal" lives. Shadowy concepts like enlightenment and samadhi stand in stark contrast to the lives we are actually living; we hear that a world of spiritual joy awaits us — somewhere between the Buddha's knowing smile and the abundant lifestyles of a beautiful few who trained at the feet of mysterious masters — but meanwhile we are bound to the routines of working, studying, having relationships, raising children, and washing the dishes. No matter how hard you try to be the unattached observer, to stand outside the stream of daily life and view it objectively, the demands of domesticity require involvement in this material world. Dinner does not cook itself. Yet popular spiritual teachers have presented everyday aspects of life — sex, food, family, work and relationships — as merely the content of your awareness training or, worse, an obstruction to it. This is a mistake. These seemingly mundane activities are themselves the all-powerful means to enjoy your reality.

As for me, I come from a long line of teachers. My mother and father were schoolteachers, and teachers of teachers. It was to this that they devoted their lives. My grandfather, too, worked a lifetime in education, providing programs in state prisons. He saw that all suffering and human mistakes happen when we are not given life's tools. He helped thousands of people to rehabilitate, to enter their lives and get out of prison. I follow in my grandfather's footsteps and I too am going to give you some essential life tools.

I was raised in the suburbs and had the usual adolescence and early life. I went dutifully through the school system, readying myself to be a productive citizen prepared to work in the universities or the factories, depending on whatever my abilities would turn out to be. Still, I sensed there had to be something more — something beyond work, duty and citizenship — for our human lives; and I became fascinated to know what made people happy or miserable. I saw that it was intimacy that was needed; and I saw that we were deprived of it by the priorities of the usual life being dished up by society. Then suddenly came the Sixties with a wild message of hope blasting through the radio Across the Universe, a world that has never been the same since. Come Together and Let it Be, we realized that All You Need is Love! And then

The Beatles went to India to study with a yogi — a fact that caught my keen attention — and they generously made their personal spiritual quest public. They poured their hearts, their hunger, questions and dreams, into rhythms and words that became our own. So, by twenty, I was in India at the feet of known and unknown masters, realizers, holders of the traditions, charlatans and the real deal. We yogis intermingled then between East and West and further brought down walls, weaving our own heavy sounds and hopes for humanity into worldwide awareness.

These people like The Beatles leveled the playing field for humanity. They directed their light onto the insidious hierarchies that had enslaved people to power structures. They remained ordinary people amidst super fame; and they treasured their own humanity, telling the world that money and stardom had not been an answer to their own suffering, that the need for love and partnership and the demands of family were no different for them than for anyone else. They robustly communicated that it meant everything to be an ordinary person, that a Working Class Hero is something to be, that you do not need to climb a social ladder to be an acceptable human being, and that no one need give you or can take away from you what you already are — a fully empowered individual and the perfect beauty of life. What I saw was that all this was really a contemporary outburst of the great spiritual traditions that had gone before. Wisdom has always been delivered on wings of music, and popular culture deserves as much attention as the great traditions of the

# "WISDOM HAS ALWAYS BEEN DELIVERED ON WINGS OF MUSIC, AND POPULAR CULTURE DESERVES AS MUCH ATTENTION AS THE GREAT TRADITIONS OF THE PAST."

past. Now in the overarching worldview we have of our vast history we can celebrate the entire wisdom tradition of humanity and all its unique appearances of culture, geography and time. Our modern conclusion is that we all share the one true life.

Whether the prison is real or metaphorical, whether the walls are built of stone or self-doubt, the lesson is about getting free with life's tools in your hands. It is my work to help people get out of the prison of society's dysfunction and denial, to claim your God-given life. It is your birthright. I will help you know what you really want and show you how to get it. Sometimes it is hard to sort out our real desires from those contrived by society. Because we are sold everything from celibacy to sex, to God or Buddhahood, beauty as asserted by Vogue or Yoga Journal. From sugar and fat to slim and green, and we don't know what we really need anymore. I will get you there.

My contention is this: What we all really want is an intimate connection to life, continuity of a loving relationship with life and sex, the power and regenerative healing force of life. And guess what? Everyone actually wants the same as you. So if you set an intention and carry out the practical means you will certainly be met by someone who needs the same thing as much as you. If you know what you really want, no power in this world can stop you from having it. The universe is conspiring to see that you get it. But if you don't know what you want or want too many things, you cannot get anything and the world will trip you up all the way!

In the conventional spiritual process of trying to attain some heightened sense of being, you can end up feeling hungrier than ever, especially when you fail to achieve or sustain some idealized state of happiness. Feeling inadequate, instead of enlightened, is the inevitable result of striving for enlightenment. Paradoxically, the very search for the idea of enlightenment creates the opposite. By implying that enlightenment is not already present you come to believe that you are lacking something you need to be truly happy and at peace. You believe that you are not good enough. You believe that you are not working hard enough. The battle for approval rages on because we've simply replaced our chains of iron for chains of gold, which are harder to get off because we are enamored by the gold: where you once questioned the measure of your bank-account, you now question the measure of your spirituality.

Seeking anything implies that you don't have it. It is only unhappiness that looks for happiness. The very action of looking for truth denies the intrinsic reality that you are the truth. You are the power of this cosmos arising as pure intelligence and beauty. So the looking is the problem. Looking implies the absence. There is no absence of truth. Your search seems to negate the truth that is you, as you already are, the present embodiment of life's wonder — a living, breathing expression of reality itself. So stop looking, start living.

We need to understand that this attitude, this impoverishment of the intrinsic integrity that is always already our own, is not necessarily true to the origins of spiritual practices. Deeply embedded in the cultures of the ancient and indigenous world is the idea of a primordial source, a power or principle lying behind absolutely everything, that takes form as the universe — as life itself — in all its detail. With no division between religion and society, sacred and secular, or creator and creation, all of life's activities were electrically charged with the immediate presence of the source. All it takes for life's activities to express and embody this truth is deep participation in the source as it manifests in all ordinary conditions. And as such, the source can be directly experienced in every way. Participation in life, not seeking in life is the secret.

This vision of the world is simple, but subtle; yet doctrines were invented that persuaded followers to search for the source, as if it were not already present in the sheer fact of existence and the very substance of everything. The outcome of this was to deny the world of our experiences and the reality of our selves in an attempt to get back to the idea of source. This has been going on for millennia; it's encapsulated in the belief that God is up there in heaven, while we struggle on down here on Earth, utterly polluted by our animal nature and needing

# "WHEN YOU STOP SEEKING, YOU CREATE AN OPPORTUNITY TO BECOME INTIMATE WITH THE DIVINE. INTIMATE WITH ALL OF LIFE AND LIFE'S CONDITIONS. INTIMATE WITH YOUR SELF. THEY ARE ALL ONE AND THE SAME."

to change our identity through the sternest purifications of mind and body before we stand a chance of getting anywhere near the divine. Today, this idea of having to search for truth is so deeply ingrained that it has become an uninspected habit, a cosmic game of hide-and-seek that we are all supposed to play.

Instead, let's look back at the original understanding that appearance and reality, source and seen, are really one. There is no difference between spirit and matter, for they are intimately related. It's like trying to separate day and night–without one, the other ceases to exist. If you think of spirit as energy, the invisible life force that flows through us all, and then consider that Einstein, Neils Bohr and others have long since proven that matter and energy are essentially different manifestations of the same thing, then you may get a clearer idea of what I'm talking about. And this idea might encourage you to re-evaluate the whole notion of seeking truth. When you stop seeking, you create an opportunity to become intimate with that truth. Intimate with the divine. Intimate with all of life and life's conditions. Intimate with your self. They are all one and the same; and they are as readily available as your body, breath, and relationship. The habit of discontent, of obsessively looking and waiting for something to happen, can be discarded altogether. When you do this, you will be free to start living in truth, living in what is. For me, that means the reality that is always upon us in every breath, every heartbeat, and in every relationship: to ourselves and to others, whether sexual or not sexual, and to all of life in all its forms. To put it simply: God is the Earth, not elsewhere.

For many generations, men have been unwilling to be with women in mutuality: mutual education, wealth, energy, social roles or sexuality. For as long as this goes on, men and women will never know themselves or touch the stars. I have observed that in every way, including sex, mutuality heals generational pain and the dysfunction inherited from our ancestors. And love allows everything that is not love to be seen and understood. So, we have no choice but to get started and continue our bodily loving. Through equal and opposite respect and absorption in each other the pain leaves us. The male-female union is the very form of the universe, reality itself. The union of opposites reveals the source of opposites, the great cosmic dynamo that powers us. We can do this for ourselves, for all future generations and even retroactively for our ancestors. By embracing our own life and sexual character, we end the pain of the past and the chain of events that must be broken.

# Yogini Marilyn and the Denial of the Feminine

Not long ago I posted on Facebook a photograph taken in 1948 that shows Marilyn Monroe (aka Norma Jean Mortenson, later Baker) doing yoga asanas that she learned from Indra Devi, who learned them from T. Krishnamacharya, the great Indian yogi known as "the teacher of teachers". The photo of Marilyn received an overwhelming response that acknowledged not only the fun connection, but also the significance of that connection. Marilyn was and is perceived as a life-sign, a deity, a Christlike sacrifice for the sins of man. She revealed the problem and the changes we must make in our own life and in society. Many women have told me that Marilyn's experience is essentially their own. Born fresh and free, wild and sexual, they became inappropriately sexualized, objectified, abused, manipulated, feared, threatened. Some, having been sexually exploited, learned to turn the tables and went on to exploit. Others were depressed or even suicidal, usually living in compromised situations pacified by media and legal or illegal drugs.

Either way, all had to go through a life crisis to claim their own life, free themselves of the sexual dysfunction of society and the predatory male, and learn how to be in relationships of mutuality, the cooperation of autonomous equals. "You lived your life like a candle in the wind. Never knowing who to cling to when the pain set in," as Bernie Taupin wrote of Norma Jean in

# "THE INSIDIOUS MANIPULATION AND DEGRADING OF THE FEMININE IS UNIVERSAL AND MUST BE CORRECTED IN OUR TIME."

the song made famous by Elton John, who sang it at the funeral of Princess Diana. I would like to have known Norma Jean too. I would like to have given yoga to her — strength receiving, inhalation exhalation — intimacy with the power of her own life. I would like to have given Marilyn intimacy with her own life prior to potential intimate connection to others. I would like to have taught yoga to her potential intimates too, so that they could learn to love their life. So that they would have known how to receive her, the wild power and beauty of the natural life, instead of needing to control, manipulate, objectify, or penetrate the feminine for some brief consoling moment.

The insidious manipulation and degrading of the feminine is universal and must be corrected in our time. It is not a simple equation, like male is wrong, female is abused. It is a vast cultural mistake based on the doctrines that have created civilization. That God or truth is "other," elsewhere" and not in the earth, not in the miracle of appearance, not in sex, not in woman, not in man. This vast mistake is, of course, the cause and fuel of fundamentalist terrorism we are suffering. The only long-term cure is education. God is in the earth,

God is in sex, the miracle of life arising. We can correct the imbalance. We can create collaboration, cooperation between the sexes. It is not about one teaching the other but just a matter of receiving the power of the other for the mutual empowerment of both — to reside in and as the source of both for the benefit of both and for the benefit of all creation. Please help me deliver this into the world on behalf of Marilyn, all women and all men.

Dear Yogini Marilyn manifested the power and vulnerability of the wild feminine that men had no idea what to do with. It finally destroyed her bodily existence. I visited her grave to pay my respects. In fear of death man attempts to create eternity and glory for himself through religious institution, property, rape of Mother Earth, and control of women. He does not come to peace with bodily existence or participate peacefully in the mystery power of the body or its passing. He therefore does not surrender to Earth and the great powers of Earth, the sublime regenerative force that is 100 percent given and constant. He does not surrender or support the wild feminine. She is enjoyed through the great nurturing polarity of male-female union within and without and is everyone's birthright. This is the primordial religious practice before man invented doctrine that dissociated him from the feminine. Man has not yet been taught to access this power of his own reality. Instead he is afraid, has vilified sex and struggles simultaneously to control it and get it. When all along it is freely given.

Dear Marilyn, long may you live and thrive on Earth.

# Yab-Yum: The Ancient Accord, Cooperation, and Mutual Empowerment of Man and Woman

Ancient Tibet had a shamanic culture called Bön before Buddhism became its dominant culture. The indigenous people had been worshiping the powers of nature for centuries. After Buddhism began to percolate into the South Tibetan region around the third and fourth centuries, the county's cultural history was increasingly affected by the meeting, confusion, and integration of these two great cultural expressions. In the early days there were bands of wild women who had no regard for the culture and formality of the male Buddhist idealists, leading to a kind of standoff. Orthodox Buddhism considered the women to be uncouth, deranged, and dangerous with their suspicious practices and strange shamanic powers. But something happened after King Trisong Detsen invited the legendary Indian yogi known as Padmasambhava to come to Tibet in the late eighth century. Padmasambhava, whose name means "Lotus-born," came from Oddiyana in Ancient India, an area today identified with the Swat Valley of present-day Pakistan. He grew fond of the wild feminine and a relationship of cooperation developed that was of mutual benefit. It was not a question of one controlling the other but rather of autonomous beings in support of each other. Padmasambhava did not try to impose a superior doctrinal point of view on these indigenous women, but they and he both found advantages in each other's company.

To this day the image of a couple in open sexual embrace is part of the spiritual iconography of Tibet that has profound meaning and purpose. From a Western perspective, it may seem surprising that images of a male and female in face-to-face sexual union, often fully naked, are commonplace and are viewed with both cultural importance and profound respect. The image is known as Yab-Yum (literally, "Father-Mother"), which represents the primordial union of wisdom and compassion. The male figure is usually linked to *karuna*, compassion, and *upaya*, or skillful means, while the female partner relates to *prajña*, or insight. It would be naïve to imagine that this is some kind of symbolism and not about the actual practice of sexual intimacy of mutuality in which these truths are found. It is also about the representation of an actual yoga of strength receiving, of inhalation-exhalation, that is required to find and embody one's male and female qualities, to go beyond the common sexual dysfunctions that society has otherwise imposed on us.

I find it disturbing, not to mention outright weird, that society in general and especially many religions still seek to control or harness the feminine. Even in so-called Tantra or Yoga teachings this misogyny is present. The only reason for this can be fear and suspicion of the wild power that is inherent in the feminine in her natural state. How much more constructive would it be to understand and embrace the obvious truth that God or

Reality is found in life's natural form, namely, the union
and cooperation of both male and female power.

My friend the birthing expert Crescence Krueger
recently wrote on this subject from her own experience:

> *"Shakti cannot be controlled, so the only thing the
> masculine can do is to surrender to the feminine.
> Then Yoga happens! Turning it around is the cause
> of a deep misogyny that distorts understanding
> of who we are, causing so much suffering in
> this world. You can become "intimate" with the
> feminine in the way much of current Tantra
> promotes, but that doesn't in itself allow yoga to
> take place either. Penetration of the feminine is
> not Tantra, even when it is with the mind. What
> is Tantra then? It is interpenetration and mutual
> receptivity. The Goddess is autonomous; she is
> already the fusion of masculine and feminine,
> consciousness and its movement; as we are.
> When two autonomous individuals come into
> the vulnerability that allows them to receive each
> other, love explodes. This is yoga. And this is the
> only constructive form of relationship in yoga.
> Our pedagogical structures and institutions
> create obstacles to the heart, in their effort to
> correct or control things. We need each other in
> mutual exchange. The enlightened teacher U.G.
> Krishnamurti was adamant that the mind must
> immerse itself in the body, not control it (as much
> spiritual doctrine insists) and I am just trying to*

*find my own way to express that verbally here:*
*Shakti is consciousness, so she doesn't need the*
*limited consciousness that the mind encompasses.*
*Its penetration of her is irrelevant. She needs*
*nothing. What the mind needs, however, is to*
*integrate into the vast intelligence of the body,*
*or Shakti, the whole/hrid/heart. Healing and*
*regeneration is the result. Enlightenment too, if*
*you want to use that word."*

The Promise Practice is an ancient spiritual tool. It is to participate in the inherent union of male and female qualities on the inside, in our own embodiment. It creates a visceral, actual change that allows us to participate in that exquisite union in the outer polarity, male to female, whether in same-sex or opposite-sex intimacy. We can do it now in this generation!

What we truly need is not secret knowledge but a realistic practice that will help us navigate through the chaos of daily life and the confusing debris of past wounds, and guide us to this source of peace and power that resides in each of us. Happiness arises when we relax into the reality of our natural condition. We can stop trying to "be here now"–we are here now. This means an intimate participation in our own lives; and it is the greatest gift we can give ourselves and everyone around us, the best model for living we can offer our children and our communities. From here, you are open and free enough to deal with whatever presents itself to you, supported by the knowledge that this intimate connection with your source of strength and truth is all that is required to feel safe and at peace.

This book is a practical, sincere guide to living that explores how and why real intimacy is as close and necessary to us as our breath is to the body, and provides not only the essential knowledge but the actual steps to embracing your real needs and desires.

Everything in these pages is established on direct personal experience:

- *the way that institutionalized culture has had a destructive impact on our sense of self and our ability to relate to others in meaningful ways;*
- *the way that these same influences have perpetuated a negative relationship to our own sexuality that has left us shying away from love;*
- *the observation that mutuality in every way, including love-making, heals the pain inherited from our ancestors;*
- *and, ultimately, the experience that the union of masculine and feminine within our own bodies and with one another is the very form of the universe that reveals the source inside us all.*

Here is the practicum, the all-purpose "how-to" manual to actualize everything that has ever inspired you or will inspire you. This is a soft message for hard times. The spiritual life is one of participation only in what already is — not an endless search. It is utter intimacy with life, here and now, with body and breath and all relationships. And you are already all of this. Now you can feel it. From this starting point, this intimacy with yourself, every other relationship is easily within your grasp. What is unimportant will naturally fall away. You will feel yourself step into your peace, power, passion and purpose, in quiet grace and certainty.

*I promise.*

"YOUR BODY
LOVES
ITS BREATH"

# PART ONE

## The Intimacy of Your Breath

To the ancient masters, a powerful physical practice was not merely a form of exercise meant to increase flexibility or fitness. It was a spiritual way of life based on the intuitive understanding that everything is arising from one nurturing source. It is direct embrace of that power. The key to the power of their practices was, and continues to be, the breath.

What is breath? It is life. It is a baby's first cry and a father's last sigh, and the mist that rises from a lake on a winter's day. It is every inconceivable force in the cosmos, the essence of all transformation and the supporting ground of all existence. It is the boundless and ineffable depth of everything we see, feel, and experience.

Your body loves its breath. When we breathe well we can feel strong and alert, and at the same time, calm and relaxed. This is the best way to be in life. And yet breathing isn't as simple as it may seem. Emotions and experience have an intense effect on the body and breath. We always respond, be it in subtle or palpably visceral ways, to every experience we have.

For example, the sight of profound beauty might leave us momentarily breathless as the body takes in a spontaneous inhale, which it then suddenly, but briefly, holds. Remarkably, it is the body's way of acknowledging that the beauty we see is the same beauty that is in

## "TO BREATHE WELL IS SIMPLY TO MOVE THE BODY IN EXACT SYNCHRONICITY WITH THE BREATH. THE BODY MOVEMENT IS THE BREATH MOVEMENT."

us, as us. When there is sadness and loss, the body will naturally sigh or exhale as its extraordinary intelligence releases obstructive emotions from its system. When we feel afraid, our breath seems to stop altogether, as we become frozen in a state of fear. This is the body's natural way of focusing its energy and becoming alert before it responds to a threat.

For many of us, the inhalation is qualitatively different from the exhalation. Most of the time, we take in short, narrow breaths that don't calm and refresh our body. Pervasive social conditioning has created a sense of separation in our minds, which causes many imaginary fears, threats, and self-doubts to arise. All this is imposed upon our perfect biological life machines. And it affects our body and breath in countless ways. We are then not breathing fully or well due to fear or trepidation, exhaling too much out of some imagined loss, inhaling too little to receive any real nourishment.

This is why it is so good to do The Promise Practice. First, to establish and remind ourselves that we are already in perfect relationship to everything, and we are wholly designed for that! And second, to consciously and intentionally move the body and breath through inhalation, exhalation, and short retentions to release the frozen patterns of breath caused by fear, anxiety and depression, all of which come from the imagined idea that we are separate entities, alone in this universe.

To breathe well is simply to move the body in exact synchronicity with the breath. The body movement is the breath movement. The inhalation is drawn from above as receptivity, and the exhalation comes from below as strength. The breath envelops the movement as a means of empowering the body and its energy in a most refined and subtle way. The breath is the movement. We breathe without struggle. Maybe a sense of work is involved, but not struggle.

When we learn The Promise Practice, it's important to start off with the breath synced to the body movement, because the power of the anatomy serves the breath. Later, when the breath is stronger, we can breathe without the body movement. But if at first we try to take deep breaths without the body movement, it can be troublesome and hard work. Not only does the breath movement offer guidance and support to the body, but the movement of the body also facilitates the deepening of the breath. All in all, the body, breath, and mind are felt to be part of a single, flowing movement. This is the life current that already runs through you, simply making itself known. An inhalation allows us to receive what is new and what we need: love, beauty, and a deepening of relationship with all that surrounds us. On exhalation we release what is old and not needed. Retaining the breath for short intervals, we become alert to the fact that we are life itself. Pausing after exhalation reveals strength, while retaining the breath at the top of an inhalation shows that we are beauty itself, receptive beings always in relationship to what is also beautiful. The breath should be smooth and unobstructed, to replace old patterns of breathing. In so doing, we release all unnecessary emotions and patterns, receiving new life and residing in alert awareness that we are alive.

## Receiving and Releasing

When we first begin The Promise Practice of moving the body in union with the breath, it is normal to find that the inhalation is somewhat tighter — shorter and shallower — than the exhalation. That's okay; and it isn't your fault. It's happening because the stress our minds and bodies have been subjected to is reflected in the breath. Look at it this way: We've all had the experience of our breath speeding up when we're feeling jittery before a job interview, or of it being deep and languorous when we're slowly waking up after a good long sleep. Now, we've had to be tough in order to survive. This strength is a defensive mechanism that puts up a wall between our own selves and external threats. It's reflected in the exhalation of the breath, pushing outward and away from our inner vulnerability, protecting our softness from harm.

For the same reason — we've had to be tough — it's hard to drop our walls, to let in tenderness and care. This distrust or lack of receptivity is reflected in the tightness of the inhalation. These two processes, inhalation and exhalation, are usually happening unconsciously; and when the inhalation is out of balance with the exhalation, it means that our bodies and minds are continually giving out a lot strength without taking much back in.

After many years of breathing this way, not only do we end up with sore shoulders and backs, but we also aren't getting enough oxygen into our systems to sleep well or maintain a good level of health. Because our bodies aren't feeling very good, our minds keep pushing outward rather than settling down and going inward. The cycle of stress continues.

Correcting the breath is an easy and pleasurable thing to do. It involves using your attention to soften into the feeling of your inhalation and exhalation, gradually lengthening both so that they are balanced and complementary. Immediately you will feel in your whole body the qualities of the inhalation and exhalation in perfect union. Not only does the breath movement offer guidance and support to the body, but the movement of the body also facilitates a deepening of the breath. All in all, the body, breath, and mind are felt to be part of a single, flowing movement. This is the life current that already runs through you, simply making itself known. The healing process has begun. With each inhalation, we draw the nourishing strength of life into this complex of mind and body. With each exhalation, we let go of the hardness of so many generations of violence against this being.

As we receive and release, we are literally healed and cleansed. Ultimately, as we soften into this natural state of affairs, one thing becomes certain: this world and this body-mind are no different. They dance in the same direction, toward growth, healing, and new life, each contributing to the other's flourishing in total intimacy.

## The Process of Healing

The process of healing and realization is in relationship with actual others. It is in the mutual intimacy between two actual people who freely choose each other. Practice of intimate relationship, including sex, is the process of all psychological adjustment, self-discovery, and under-standing. In relationship we release what is not needed to receive what is needed. The natural flow of feelings from anger to its cause, pain; to grief; to compassion and forgiveness is enacted and practiced in that order. The next more basic emotion is predicted and permitted. Practitioners learn to speed this process, and the over-whelming whole body-heart connection to all things is understood to be the point of human life. Love brings up everything that is unlove to be seen and understood. So the process of relationship can be disturbing, as all of society's dysfunction and the pain in one's family lineage is released.

And so, the practical means of practicing intimacy need to be supplied. Our world is full of spiritual and psychological processes that do not fulfill this most fundamental need. It is shocking how so many great spiritual teachers never even mention sex and relationship, or acknowledge it as the basic method of transformation. Such teachers are often seen as the model of human attainment, so their sexlessness is passed on as the norm or regarded as a superior state. On the other side of the problem, so-called tantric or "sacred" sex teachers sell exaggerations, false desires and public confusion without giving the practical means of a real yoga, an intimate union with life via body, breath, and relationship, in that order. Whether it is new or old world religion, mindfulness meditation, popularized yoga, dance, shamanic medicine ceremonies, or the myriad offerings of our secular world, scant training exists for successful intimacy and sexuality. Nor is there acknowledgment that intimacy with all ordinary conditions including male-female intimacy (same sex or opposite sex) is the means to know reality or "God." In fact, the usual spiritual offerings teach processes for the individual's internal reveries that result in dissociation from all ordinary conditions. Such cultures created society's sex dysfunction in the first place. These practices belong in the context of a robust prior practice of intimate connection. Otherwise they cause delusion and separation.

∞

## Exercise One: Strength/Receiving Meditation

Quietly sitting in an upright posture, please notice that your body base and spine completely support your soft crown above.

Feel how your head is held erect by the strength of your spine. In fact, the whole front of your body including your arms and hands is supported by this masterful strength that moves upward from your body base.

When you observe nature's body mechanics you can see that the crown and front is built only for relationship, the hands for holding, the arms for embracing, the crown for receiving and processing perceptions.

The mouth tastes and absorbs nutrients that are processed in our soft bellies. The whole front of the body is also soft and receptive. The human species learned to stand upright with this soft frontal line and feeling skin. It is one whole system of strength that is utterly soft and receptive.

This amazing body and brain holds mind and preceptors, the eyes that can see and the ears that hear, the skin that feels. It is a receiving mechanism of unparalleled power.

What a wonder!

# Delores's Story:
# Learning to Breathe

I know a wonderful doctor who works hard for her patients and her worldwide community. Like so many people, Dolores was sacrificing her own health for the sake of others. She did not know any other way because her parents had drummed into her at an early age that what was most important was hard work and career success. She could carry the stress in her early career but as time went on she began to develop health issues, including adrenal deficiency, exhaustion, and anxiety. In conversation with Delores, I discovered that she was depressed because all the ways that she had used to be able to keep her spirits high were now failing her. She even found that some of her favorite activities, such as marathon running, skiing, and hiking she could no longer do without experiencing extreme fatigue. Also, the fun that she used to have dining out and drinking fine wines and liquors only made matters worse. Yet her workload and responsibilities never diminished.

She genuinely did not know how to stop and care for herself as well as for others, her first and most creative calling. As we talked, she came to understand that if she didn't take care of herself she would never be able to take care of others. I told her, "Put your own oxygen mask on first." Dolores felt the logic of that. She also understood that the challenges she once loved were no longer appropriate for her, so she stopped running marathons and working to be the best at everything, and began to engage in activities that would give her energy rather than deplete her.

I explained to her how all forms of life have two essential qualities: an absolutely strong aspect, (which she had developed so impeccably through her hard work and athletic activities) and an absolutely soft and receptive aspect, (which she had not developed at all). Each aspect depends upon the other to ensure the survival and integrity of the whole system. Look at a tree: There is the magnificently strong trunk that culminates and supports delicately soft, juicy foliage, which receives nutrients from above. Without the roots and trunk there can be no foliage. Without the leafy green above, the trunk will wither and die. It is one intelligent system functioning as extreme intelligence and perfection that is life. This is how we are, too.

Reflecting on this, Dolores understood that she needed to develop her soft, receptive side while still nurturing her strength. My prescription for her was simple: Move and Breathe. I told her, "Exhalation is your strength, and inhalation is literally your ability to receive and be nurtured."

Like most people, when Delores took an inhalation she would do so with a strong muscular effort. As she tried hard to suck in air with a sniffing sound, her nostrils would tighten. I told her about Dr. Mark Pian, a Pediatric Pulmonologist at Rady Children's Hospital in San Diego, California, whose pertinent line, "Inhalation doesn't suck," means that it's cool to inhale. It makes you feel better. But more than that, he is explaining that the inhalation is not a literal "sucking" process, which would require a difficult muscular effort. In fact, it is the opposite of effort, as inhalation occurs by making space in the lung cavity; a vacuum is created when the pressure of the outside atmosphere pushes the air through, gratefully and gracefully, into the lungs. As you move your arms over your head, the rib cage and intercostal muscles expand readily and inhalation comes easily. Rather than controlling the air at the nostrils, we subtly move it to the throat, to allow the larynx to become the control center of every inhalation and exhalation; you are already familiar with this as it is the way your body breathes naturally when you fall asleep. You might discover this just at the point when you drift off to sleep. Or listen to how someone lying next to you will breathe, or how a newborn baby breathes directly to and from her spine.

After I explained all this to Delores, I then instructed her to gently move her arms in exact synchronicity with her breath. She began to receive her inhalation without effort, and exhaled with masterful strength by drawing from the base of her spine. She discovered a sense of the exhalation as being powered from her base and the inhalation as being drawn in receptivity from above. She also learned how the breath should envelop the movement, when it begins just before and ends just after the movement. Soon she felt like her whole body was breathing. She said it was like sailing. "My body feels like a boat with a sail and my breath is the breeze. Off I go, effortlessly!"

At the conclusion of the practice, she reclined on the floor and rested. She then noticed something remarkable. Her body was able to rest completely. She felt a noticeable stillness within her whole body and the surrounding environment. Yet energy seemed to be flowing through her, rendering a feeling of alertness. This is what I mean when I say it's important to leave the body alone and give it a chance for its inherent intelligence to function, so that its innate wellbeing and balance can return.

Delores learned to enjoy the time each day when she would engage in breathing practice while moving her body, and then consciously rested for as long as she liked. Sometimes it felt so pleasurable to her that she would rest for quite long periods. She also noticed that a profound feeling of connection to her own body and life began to arise. This spilled over into her physical connection to others, especially her partner, as well as her patients and all her friends and family. Delores began to relax into life, and experienced it more as a healing and restorative process. She found that she could now work in a way that was active and strong, yet she could stay soft, relaxed, and receptive as she went about her business. Work did not wear her out like before.

By deliberately breathing more consciously and matching the receptive, feminine inhalation with the strong, masculine exhalation, what Dolores experienced firsthand is the effect that ultimately comes when the male-female polarities of the breath are fully balanced, integrated, and unified.

## Exercise Two: Inhale/Exhale

1. Sit comfortably on the floor with legs crossed or on a chair with your feet flat on the floor.

2. Place one hand on your chest, one hand on your lower belly.

3. Close your eyes and focus on your upper hand and chest.

4. Inhale through your nose while making a 'aahh' sound in the back of your throat and feel your chest rise. Keep your lips lightly sealed.

5. Now, bring your focus to your lower hand.

6. Exhale with an 'hahh' sound at the back of your throat and feel your belly flatten and firm.

7. Repeat a number of times until it becomes a natural, easy process of inhaling from above, exhaling from below. This is receptivity and strength in equal balance.

"THE POWER, INTELLIGENCE, BEAUTY, AND CREATION OF THIS INFINITE UNIVERSE ARE BASED ON ONE PRINCIPLE: THE MUTUAL ATTRACTION OF OPPOSITES IN UNION."

# The Union of Opposites

The power, intelligence, beauty, and creation of this infinite universe are based on one principle: the mutual attraction of opposites in union. At every level this is how things work. In the starry mystery of sky, suns, moons, and planets are held by each other in perfect balance and ever-moving alignments. At the tiniest atomic level we observe positive and negative poles in perfect union, holding unimaginable power and the steady beauty of all material form. And in all of life forms, too, this principle is operating. Look at a flower: What is really going on there? It is the perfect exchange of the male female chemistries, the necessary exchange that creates new life and which ensures every species' continuity and evolutionary perfect adaptation in the eternal nurturing flow of life. We are this system in our very substance and structures of body and mind. This ease in full participation in the polarity of opposites is the secret to our personal power, longevity, health, and happiness. It cannot be by-passed. It is as simple as in the natural body balance of all the opposites, and in the special empowerment of the breath's strength and receptivity, where the male female opposites of life are permitted to function. Then we become capable of the polarity of inner to outer in the mutual embrace of someone we choose. Here the nurturing power of the universe flows and we discover the ancient secrets of human wisdom presently manifesting in our very own embodiment.

Man has never really looked up from the swamp and seen

the beauty and safety of his natural world. Still burdened with fear, he struggles with male force alone to protect himself and to overcome an imagined threat. The body and the mind become bound, apparently strong and armored, but they are not receptive. Sometimes it is hard to convince strong yet frightened people to breathe in without a struggle. But it is worth persisting, for when they do it is a pure joy for them. This action of moving the body to facilitate an inhalation is the particular way that bound men and women can take an inhalation without drama, without a struggle as pure receptivity. Here is the pure joy of their feminine quality. Here they can feel the natural state as the perfect power of the cosmos arising as all polarity, as self and all form.

The most fundamental purpose of moving postures is to facilitate the union of the male and female qualities of life, which are enacted by the breath moving in exact synchronicity with the body movement. This merge of the exhalation with the inhalation enacts the function of strength that is entirely receptive, which the essential reason to practice yoga. Asana uses the anatomy of the whole body to facilitate this purpose, which then empowers breathing in stationary posture, i.e., pranayama. Therefore, asana can be defined as "moving pranayama." The importance of asana is its energetic function, not what it looks like. What the practitioner actually feels is primary. How the asana looks outwardly is of secondary importance. Asana is principally a process of integrating body, breath and mind. It isn't there for its own sake. It facilitates pranayama. If pranayama is successful, the mind will be made clear and the body energized; then meditation, also known as dhyana in Sanskrit, spontaneously and easily arises. No technique in yoga exists for its own sake. This perfect union of above with below, inhalation with exhalation, strength with receptivity, reveals the heart, the source and power of life.

Life consists of opposites in union. This is how the universe operates. Through the union of the male and female aspects of life, new life is regenerated and nurtured and the substance of all existence is sustained. In the natural state, male is the strength of life, which always includes the feminine aspect of receptivity. Without one pole the opposite cannot, does not exist. If we live as if only strength is all that is important without its opposite quality of receptivity, strength becomes brittle and soon degenerates and destroys itself. Unfortunately, in our social environment we behave as if life is always about being strong, capable, and penetrating of the world. This is no small problem, and it causes peril in our health and relationships, and all of life is now at risk because of it.

Male and female qualities are present as the essential nature of all opposites, such as left and right, above and below, dark and light, inhalation and exhalation. The breath teaches us that although there are opposites, these distinct phenomena are not at all opposed in any way. Rather, they are polar and mutual. Nothing is exclusive, and nothing exists as isolated or in separation from the whole. Masculine aspects such as strength and logic are counterbalanced by the feminine aspects of gentleness and intuition, and are interdependent and work in an ongoing and delicate synchronicity with one another. Like an acrobat whose muscles on the left and right sides of her body flux continuously to prevent her from falling off a high wire, in an effective union of opposites the drawing from both polarities is a seamless, balanced exchange. In Chinese philosophy this interaction of opposing energies is known as Yin (feminine) and Yang (masculine), and represents the juxtaposition and continuous interplay of opposing dynamic forces of the universe.

Yet when doubt, fear, or insecurity come into play, our physical and psychological wellbeing becomes stressed and imbalance occurs; discomfort, disorder, or disease then takes hold and new patterns, albeit dysfunctional ones, may be established. For the breath, this can happen at the most rudimentary and unconscious level. Through the essential function of inhalation and exhalation, the breath sustains our very existence and is responsive to the body and mind.

Sometimes people that seem to be strong turn out to be not strong at all. Often an early degenerative illness can develop or even an untimely sudden death will occur when something sadly breaks in the system. We become habituated in our society to stressful activity and conventionally "being strong," but aren't really strong because we lack receptivity. Real strength is always integrated with receptivity. Sometimes the strongest among us in all their business just cannot seem to take the time to relax and receive, to take a steady comfortable inhalation. Yet those who shoulder responsibility for others must be given the opportunity for health and relaxation. Care givers of all kinds, first responders, police, politicians, artists and working people of every stripe must be given the natural ability to receive. It must be taught to them. Otherwise, we are asking for tragedy that sadly we already know too well.

## Exercise Three: Breath & Body Movement

1. Stand with your feet hip width and arms relaxed at your sides.

2. Inhale into your chest and raise your arms overhead, allowing the breath movement to be slightly longer than the body movement.

3. Exhale, flattening your belly as you lower your arms back to your sides. Again, allow the length of the breath to be slightly longer than the movement of your arms.

4. Repeat a number of times until you get the feeling that the movement of your arms is enveloped by each part of your breath.

# The Loss of Receptivity

Receptivity is vitally important, yet most of us don't appreciate how disabled we are when lacking it. On a most basic level, receptivity is responsiveness, a taking-in, an acceptance of something offered. It is an observance of what is available, both seen and unseen, an openness, a trust. It is the essential quality of the feminine, and allows us to draw sustenance from all around us. To be receptive at last allows us to relax into and feel our natural state. It enables the energy of life to flow freely through us and to others around us. The body and mind become healthy and relaxed. We stop reacting to stress, which is the one illness that causes all other illnesses. The body needs a chance for its natural and inherent intelligence to function and regenerate, and will do so automatically in the absence of stress.

The inhalation is literally the receptive action of life. The body breathes in! It receives! It is easy to learn and practice how to inhale deeply and fully, and this has radical effects on all our other behavior. It is a visceral and practical means to developing that natural aspect of life that is receptive, and at least half of the equation that is life. At the present time as in the past, however, there has been an undervaluing of what we regard as feminine qualities: emotional openness, softness, and most important, the ability to receive and operate from a position of love. But these qualities must not be mistaken as belonging to women alone; they are inherent in everyone. Yet a capacity for receptivity has been overlooked,

# "RECEPTIVITY IS THE ESSENTIAL QUALITY OF THE FEMININE, AND ALLOWS US TO DRAW SUSTENANCE FROM ALL AROUND US."

if not forgotten, by most of us, a consequence of complex and powerful socio-cultural forces and beliefs that deemed the feminine weak and suppressed it in infinite ways over the centuries. A denial of the feminine began with primitive man, who saw nature as a wild and unpredictable threat to human survival. Ways and means were found to ensure the survival of humankind amidst a dangerous universe. An idea arose that the more a society cleaved to the notion of order, the greater the benefit for all involved. Then, as now, we are conditioned to believe that our wellbeing depends on such order, and only by means of some cultivated movement away from our earthy, biological nature (the feminine and her attendant qualities) can we realize the higher goods that culture promises, be it entry into heaven, finding love, getting married, or a host of other things. Yet to the extent that each and every one of us is born of a mother and a father, all beings arise from and embody a perfect intertwining of masculine and feminine. Men and women alike have suffered from the denial of the feminine — an entire half of our already-established connection to life itself, half of each person's capacity to experience and to respond to every situation.

This historical suppression of feminine qualities has

# "THE INHALATION IS LITERALLY THE RECEPTIVE ACTION OF LIFE. THE BODY BREATHES IN! IT RECEIVES!"

created a cultural environment in which only masculine qualities are reflected in our personal relationships, both with self and others, and in our benchmarks of success. When the masculine is perceived as separate from, and even opposed to, the feminine, the capacity to be receptive is deeply compromised. Strength becomes oriented toward outwardly assertive displays of force, as softness is considered to be weakness. Yet strength that is not synchronistic with receptivity or softness degenerates and destroys itself. Men are not taught how to receive the powers of women, but to merely and fearfully control them. Yet our sensual physicality and fundamental needs continue to display an intrinsic connection to nature. As such, our bodies have the power to cut through cultural illusions and reveal us at our most vulnerable and powerful. It is at this most basic level that our relationship to nature — and the healing of our sense of separation from the world around us — can be restored.

As we push out and away from ourselves our sense of self comes to rest more on the perceived achievement of external goals and less on the simple feeling of connection with all manifestations of life. It becomes increasingly difficult for us to receive the tender strength that is already there in the world around us, in others, and, ultimately, in ourselves. We are exhausted by our efforts, rather than nurtured. Like shallow breathing, we operate from a space of contraction, rather than realizing the depth and potential that our natural functioning allows.

## Strength Receiving

We imagine the mind to have a life of its own because it can think. The mind is in fact a function of the whole body and in its natural state is infused with the extreme intelligence that is life. The quality and functioning of the mind is the same as the whole body, the same as life itself. The power of The Promise Practice is that it links the mind to the body, to its source, and imbibes it with life's intelligence, beauty and the fundamental male-female nature of life — strength that is receptive. We go beyond the hither to imagined identities in the mind and feel directly the vast source of our real nature, reality itself. When this link to life is made you will taste life like never before. No disturbance in the mind can touch this vast pristine reality you know yourself to be. You live in this world in intimate relationship to everything, as life, not as a complicated "subject" to complicated "objects." All that limited identity and assumption about yourself and others dissolves. You are the power of the cosmos appearing as pure intelligence, beauty and function. That is all. In the embrace of any object we know the source, we know the knower, we know ourselves, consciousness, and reality itself.

How does it work? When the breath is linked to the whole body movement, the mind automatically follows the breath. The mind links to the whole body and the whole body is life. So the intelligence that is life goes into the mind. The mind is made clear and imbued with the qualities and beauty of life. We learn to use the mind intelligently as an entirely life-supportive instrument. We experience life as it is and not how we imagine it to be before the mind was linked to its source. This power will develop progressively and at some point there is a full and final clarification that life is one great nurturing reality appearing as everything.

The mind too is both a strength and receiving mechanism, the body's navigation system. The mind arises from the whole body and is a part of the whole body, its function and survival. The body's nervous system spreads to every part, channeled through the central spine, its core fluid ever increases upward until it culminates as the brain core above. The mind is the nervous system and an elaboration of its function. It is the great perceiving and intelligence of the whole body. The mind too is designed entirely and only for relationship. When it duplicates the body's natural state the mind is both utter strength and receptive in perfect synchronicity. The mind does not have a life or identity of its own! Imagining that it does is humanity's problem. It is only a mechanism and expression of the whole body, head to toe. It is an expression of the mystery, power, intelligence, beauty and function of life itself. The mind perceives all that and communicates all that. We are the wonder of existence perceiving the

# "IT IS IMPOSSIBLE TO SAY WHERE STRENGTH ENDS AND RECEPTIVITY BEGINS."

wonder of existence. We humans have a special opportunity to realize this to be so. When you link the breath to the whole body the extreme intelligence that is life comes into the mind, informs the mind of the truth of all situations and the appropriate action to take in all situations. The mind's primary function is to communicate and enjoy the power of immeasurable reality. Investigate this feeling of connectedness and love. Here is a science that conventional science has not yet touched.

Sitting here I ask you to inspect where the strength of your system is and where the soft receptive quality is. After a while you might notice that it is impossible to say where strength ends and receptivity begins. That's because it is one completely integrated system, feeling and strong, durable and flexible, male and female in one whole body-mind. In the natural state the body has strength and elasticity, always adjusting and adapting to the world around. This body is an extraordinary intelligence. It is always precisely interrelated with the rest of the universe on which it depends and to which it contributes.

You can see how all life in both the plant and animal kingdoms has these combined qualities of strength receiving. Look at a bird effortlessly in flight supported by the might of air currents across its wing. Yet that wing is so soft and receptive, ever adjusting to the needs of flight. A tree with its masterful trunk and soft foliage absorbing nutrients from above is a model too of life's strength that is receptive. As are all plants in perfect adaptation to life. We too have this arrangement in us, as us.

It is all good and functioning beautifully in the natural state as Mother Nature intends. But mankind has assumed a separation from our own reality. We have been socialized with a mental and emotional aberration that imagines that we are separate from nature and that male can be separate from female. It is simply not true. You cannot have a left without right, above without below, inhalation without exhalation, male without female. But we live as if that is possible. It is impossible to have strength without receptivity. We have dreamed up a mind dissociated from the whole body and reality itself. We attempted to control nature and the feminine, overdeveloped our male strength and underdeveloped our feminine receptivity. We got better and better at control, acquisition and looking strong. But it is a very weak strength as it turns out. Strength that cannot receive destroys itself. We see this in degenerative illness caused by stress, which is strength without receptivity. The ultimate expression of this illness is war. So strength must receive to survive and endure. Man must receive woman and vice versa. Our social and spiritual models of invincible womanless man do not suffice, typified by the man of the monastery who resides as the witness only, no longer embracing his own nature. No, man must participate in

*The Sri Chakra, an ancient symbol of strength-receptivity*

the fullness of life to be truly spiritual, to be living in and as truth, reality, consciousness. Imagine if the Pope had a wife of equal and opposite status and visibility. Likewise, the Dalai Lama. What culture might we have built?

The Promise Practice corrects the situation and delivers us from this social imprint that denies fifty percent of out natural character. It is perfect participation in all the polarities of life, including strength that is perfectly receiving, the male surrender to the feminine. Surrender is a tricky word because it implies defeat. So it might be better to say that we "receive" the feminine. Nevertheless, because centuries of male denial of the feminine, it is our special responsibility now to receive the feminine. It is a good deal for men as well because it brings them vibrant health and the certainty of the vast reality appearing as all life.

There is only reality appearing as every "thing" including all apparent limitations. There is great comfort in this understanding of the one absolute condition. The All is in all and the All is all, in the one indivisible union of love bliss.

This practice returns you to perfect participation in that. You are not the troubled person looking for God in the myriad of male methods of priesthoods and power structures of all kinds. You are God. God is appearing as you. And there are two aspects of you because everything comes into life via this mysterious union of opposites, male and female. By this union, your mother and father were formed and the nurturing flow of life created and presently sustains you. You have the strong male aspect like the sun, bright and certain. And you have the female aspect, cool calm and relaxing like the moon. There is ancient language for this union, *hatha yoga*, the union of sun (*ha*) and moon (*tha*). We participate in both. One moves the other. One strengthens the other and the nurturing forces flow through you from the place of perfect union of these polarities, the heart. Via the union of opposites, the source of opposites is revealed: the heart. From here the nurturing life energy flows through the whole body in all directions like a flower in full bloom from its heart source.

Once this practice of participating in the opposites is established, you will become strength that is receptive in your body and mind. Then spontaneously will arise your ability to be intimate with all others, and with an intimate partner, as strength that is receptive. That is to

# "THE PROMISE PRACTICE IS A TECHNOLOGY THAT ALLOWS THE HEAD TO ACKNOWLEDGE AND FEEL ITS SOURCE — THE HEART."

be present and giving to them, while at the same time receiving them in an infinite exchange.

Of course, you live in a society of restrictions. Even in your own family lineage there are all kinds of obstructions to life that have gone into you. Its okay! These go. And you can do it. This is the first generation that is able to completely finish with the patterns of the past. You can do it for yourself, your ancestors and all future generations. You will be able to review your life and go back to heal all of your personas of the younger you that were traumatized, which still seem to affect the present. You did your best in all circumstances and you came through. The mature survivor is here now. You now know love and heal all past wounds, in yourself, your parents and ancestors. Celebrate the whole of your life from procreation to now. Your parents did in fact love you absolutely as the Life they are, but they too were burdened by society's dysfunction. So you may visualize them in the perfect loving embrace and care of you and of each other. This is their natural state and this visual will take the trauma from you. Let yourself be loved as a parent naturally does. Give this to your self, and "for-give" yourself, your parents, your ancestors and all people.

Do it for everyone. Claim your life.

## Vital Energy and Flow

In life itself there is a nurturing force that is inherent and always functioning. It is intrinsic to reality. It is there in the moment of conception and it is here right now, sustaining us, nurturing all of us throughout our entire lives. Even in death this nurturing flow is present. By cultivating awareness of this sustenance we come to see that we are always completely loved, always uncon- ditionally nurtured by life itself. That is why when we engage fully in life, we feel sustained. By participating in the male-female qualities of life within our own bodies as well as without, we permit this miraculous nurtur- ing force to move freely and without constraint. Is it not amazing how this nurturing force is operating, despite our stressful, destructive behaviors? Life keeps pumping away, and gets us upright and moving on again, breath- ing and laughing under the sun.

We start out as one cell. In the great tradition of yoga this is known as "the heart," the *hrid*. It is the union of two ancient Sanskrit syllables: *hr*, to give, and *id*, to receive. Already established in that heart are male and female qualities. It soon grows into a whole spine and the whole body in all its masterful function. It is the source where the nurturing force flows. It is also known as the source whence all opposites arise and return.

When we practice The Promise, we can feel this nur- turing flow throughout our whole body. Sometimes we can sense it specifically flowing from our heart center. It can feel like a flower blooming in all directions into the

# "IN LIFE ITSELF THERE IS A NURTURING FORCE THAT IS INHERENT AND ALWAYS FUNCTIONING. IT IS INTRINSIC TO REALITY."

whole body like spirals of nurturing. We are really allowing the whole body to participate in and experience that nurturing flow.

Built into The Promise Practice is a technology that allows the head to acknowledge and feel its source — the heart — and allows the body to participate more fully with the heart. The strength of the body base and spine are permitted to serve the heart's purpose, that is, to extend and expand that nurturing flow of all life. The head, brain core, and thinking mind are then enabled to also serve the heart's purpose.

The Promise Practice optimizes personal and public health, if we will only do it. The technique is simply to lower the head to the heart at the top of the inhalation as that is the shortest distance between the forehead and the heart, gently stretching the back of the spine and neck. And at the end of the exhalation we lift the abdominals in and up. This is the strength of the body serving the heart's purpose.

The nurturing source and force of life flows from the heart into the whole spine through a system called chakras. These are centers of concentrated life energy arrayed up and down the body, from base to crown. There are seven commonly known, but there are more,

114 in all. When we lift the body base into the heart, the nurturing flows more effectively there. When we lower the head to the heart the nurturing flows more effectively there, too. It is the most healthy and enjoyable thing that you can do for your life.

In effect, it is like making love with life. The strength or male aspect of your body, the base and spine, learns how to be fully merged and receptive with the female aspect of your life, the soft receptive crown and front of the body including the arms. Then we are capable of fully merging with another in the same way; then the energy of life flows through all relationships, including intimate personal relationships. It is simple, and it is beautiful.

This same nurturing power also exists in your very breath, and in the combination of breath and movement that is the heart of The Promise Practice. Contradictory as it may seem, the practice is more a path of relaxation than of action, relaxing into what life is. It is a catalyst that releases all of your potential. Think of a piece of cork held down by a large rock at the bottom of a lake. When you remove the rock, the cork will simply bob to the surface of its own accord. Similarly, the Promise removes obstructions to your experience of happiness and peace, allowing these qualities to fill your entire being. What manifests when you undertake the practice may be subtle or dramatic, but it is entirely personal. It is your gift to yourself.

∞

WHEN WE ENGAGE IN THE PROMISE PRACTICE,
THE ENERGY OF LIFE FLOWS THROUGH ALL RELATIONSHIPS.
IT IS SIMPLE, AND IT IS BEAUTIFUL.

# PART TWO

## Ordinary Extraordinary:
## Intimacy with Life in All its Forms

You are here to enjoy your Life. You are here to be intimate with Life in every way, in all its forms. You are here to get your Life right. And as you are one with Life, you therefore are always intrinsically intimate with Life. Even though in the natural state your body is a peaceful organism, the mind imagines you to be separate from Life and from others. The Promise is a foolproof way of dealing with this conundrum. Not by conventional meditation — at war with your negative thoughts until you become war-weary and find a little bit of peace — but by the intimate embrace of what is already true of you. Your mind will no longer make this assumption of separation from what is real. You will be free.

Please consider this: Your body is an extraordinary intelligence functioning in complex yet refined ways. The biochemical, energetic mechanics of Life and light are keeping you well, always correcting, always healing and regenerating you in a profoundly empathetic relationship with the natural world. Your mind is arising as part of this multidimensional system of perfect relatedness. Yet you are even more than this wonder. You are Life itself, the still point, the hub, the indefinable, gracious "existing-ness": Reality itself from which the body

# "THE MIND IS NOT THE ENEMY, BUT PART OF THE WONDER AND BEAUTY AND SUPREME INTELLIGENCE THAT IS LIFE. MIND DOES NOT NEED TO BE CONQUERED IN SOME HEROIC SPIRITUAL ENTERPRISE."

and mind spring forth. Mind is a function of the whole body, and the culmination point of the whole body is the heart, the first cell of Life from which your mind arises and Life's nurturing energy flows. The mind is an extraordinary elaboration of an extraordinary nervous system. It is there as the body's navigation system in life and a communication mechanism of Life. It is how we experience Life. Mind has no existence of its own without its source. We imagine that mind has an existence of its own but this is a temporary mirage or apparition.

The mind is not the enemy, but part of the wonder and beauty and supreme intelligence that is Life. Mind does not need to be conquered in some heroic spiritual enterprise. The only thing needed is a practical means to link the mind to its source. There can be no real dissociation from Life. There is only reality itself in which every "thing" is arising. There is no limitation. There is only "apparent" limitation. That too would not exist if reality, or life as we know it, did not exist. Mind is creating a mirage of limiting identity (thought and emotional structures that have no basis in actuality). That limiting structure may be intentionally dismantled or seem to dissolve by grace once it is known to be unnecessary. There is no evil, no devil, no demons, no ego, and no separate mind. These are only the mind imagining dissociation from what is real. There is only Life, only love bliss, only vast union or dependent connectedness to all appearance and the source of all. The all is in all. The all is all.

You are at one with your own reality always and in all ways! Imagine the growth rings within a tree, a series of concentric and closely related circles. Each progressively larger ring encompasses the one that comes before it and gives shape and substance to the one that comes after. Some rings are bright and balanced, some are flimsy or unclear, and some meander, and others are evenly spaced. Every tree is unique, but two things are certain. First, whatever their characteristics, the rings do not belong to different trees, but speak of one tree with its personal seasons of challenge and growth. Second, as they spiral around a common point of origin, that heartwood that is the common center of them all suffuses each ring. In the masterful words of the poet T. S. Eliot, it is here, at the still point of the turning world, that we find their vital nucleus. Because they exist only in relation to this innermost (*intimus*) heart, each concentric ring is a relationship defined by how close it is to the core. The internal wellbeing of the heartwood determines whether the tree's growth is nourished and abundant, excessive or depleted as it reaches from inside out between earth and sky, strong in masculine trunk and utterly soft and receptive in feminine foliage. One system.

When we review our imagined tree, it ceases to be quite so imaginary. Each of us is a vital center that stands — pulsating body, breath and mind — at the core of our experiences of being-in-the-world. Like those growth rings encircling the heartwood on which they depend, our relationships with others form layers that circle us and turn outwards in embrace of the world. And if we are the heartwood, our hearts are the still-point, the invisible but felt location of the unwavering depth of our connectedness with Life itself. It is true that we live from the heart. For it is here, in this place that the ancients knew as *hrdaya*, (*hr*, to give, *da* to receive) that boundless Life surges up in unique and myriad formations with every first glimmer of cellular activity. The heart is the divine anchor of our being, radiating throughout and beyond our physical form in the shape of relationship and the truth that there is no such thing as separation. We are a factual manifestation of abundance, intelligence, and beauty. You are That — Truth incarnate and ever-present.

Everything is tangibly connected. "Intimacy" is the only fitting description of this profound state of affairs. Because the simple fact of our inseparability from Life insists that all things are brought inward (from the Latin, *intimus,* meaning "inmost"), and known familiarly through nothing less than the very structures of our own being, we are intimate. We are born, live, breathe and die in intimacy itself. Here is something worth considering. Intimacy is basically a word for being. It means that one thing is brought in so close to another that a transaction occurs, an interaction of identities like the transfer of information between cells. Although each one is unique, it is only in the context of this relationship, this polarity, that their uniqueness can ever be accurately known. For example you cannot have a "left" without a "right." There is no such thing as left without right, yet by the left the right is known and understood and vice versa. One aspect identifies and strengthens the other. Taken out of this context, each is drained of its life-force and impact, much like a stuffed animal in a museum collection — cotton-wool or glass marbles can never replace what happens in the meeting of heartbeat and eyes, the sensory expansion of encountering a fox on your daily stroll (trust me, the fox feels you as strongly as you do him or her). The reality of this contact is utterly internal, a flood of awareness running through our being. It literally and biologically touches us at the innermost level.

   Just as we can empower our relationships with the sensitivity of this internal awareness and feeling (the heartwood), our external relationships (the growth-rings) flow reciprocally and inform the quality and substance of whatever it is that we receive back into ourselves in return. Both our relationships to ourselves and to others have the potential to nourish and magnify — or limit and retard — the healing course of Life throughout our entire being. From within to without and vice versa, these movements exist together as an honest expression of being alive. Like our beautiful tree, the sparks of Life inside rise in connection with the conditions that surround us. The utter marriage of self and cosmos, the fullness of the participation of each in the other, is all that is needed for both to flourish. And this, perhaps, is our best definition of intimacy yet.

Believe me when I say it's not as complicated as it sounds. Just think of the coming of summer: as solar rays penetrate our atmosphere and warm the land with longer hours of sunlight, the heat enters all the skins of the Earth — human and non-human, plants, animals, and soil — and creates changes in how we live out what we are feeling. Just as leaves unfurl to draw in nutrients, our human minds become more wakeful, and there is a greater presence of animal activity around us. The exposure to light increases our alertness, happiness, and calmness. Our immunity strengthens. As our internal chemistry adjusts to the heat, our external behavior reflects that adaptation, and the way it makes us feel goes on to inform our sense of self and perceptions of the season. Finally, we can't separate our internal feeling from what's happening around us. The outside and inside swirl together to give rise to the wholeness of it all; and that boundary between internal and external, self and other, you and me and sun, moon and starlight, looks less like a solid wall than it does an open corridor of light, of being. The experience of summer, like the encounter with the fox, enters me, into my self, becomes familiar, and is externalized in my spontaneous self-expression. It's purely intimate. Every happening arises from the marriage of Life with life. This is not a philosophical assertion. It's just the way it works.

Intimacy, then, is more than a mere word. In this modern environment of global commoditization and a fast-food attitude to spirituality and healing, intimacy is one thing that can't be bought or sold. It is not some exaggerated ideal, or something culturally specific, or even an external goal to chase after. You just can't market intimacy like some ancient secret or esoteric relic to be auctioned off at the local New Age bookstore. In fact, it can't really even be made into a theory, because that would suggest that it was some sort of mental abstraction — and we already know that intimacy only exists in the happening of our embodied lives. And as for all the talk of self-transformation? No amount of detoxing, oil-pulling, green smoothies, meditation retreats or standing on your head is going to make you any more intimate. Learning Latin or Sanskrit is not going to make you any more intimate. Ecstatic dance or shamanic journeys are not going to make you any more intimate. No thing is going to make you any more intimate, because intimacy is not an upshot of any amount of change. When it comes to intimacy, the man driving the garbage truck and the holy-man living by the holy Ganga River, are equally endowed. There's just nothing that needs to be done — except relax in the understanding that intimacy is always already here. It is our natural state and the way of being alive in this world.

So the question is not whether you are intimate. You certainly are, and utterly so. Remember: intimacy is a description of being. The question is: Are you experiencing intimacy? Are you living out intimacy through

your actions and interactions, feeling deeply connected
to your life, your partner, and your self? For most human
minds intimacy isn't being felt as a personal reality. I
think we can state confidently that what's driving countless millions of people to seek drug and alcohol numb-
ing, psychiatry, psychology, religion and other forms
of consolation is specifically not the sense of profound
belonging and support that intimacy brings. The incal-
culable accumulated trauma of the past millennia has
colored our survival instincts. Our sapient humaneness
and the incredible cultural achievements that define us
are undercut by our status as the most dangerous species on the planet, the most prolific parasite capable of
causing death on an unprecedented scale. The sublim-
ity of our creative celebration of Life never did sit easily against our utter devastation of the world that is our
home; and at the present time, the painful questions that
arise from this conflict have become increasingly difficult to avoid as news and images of climate chaos, war,
genocide, deforestation, and abuse everywhere enter our
awareness on a daily basis via the media.

As the massive global political forces at play feel
uncontainable and threaten to overwhelm our individual power, we question our dreams and constrain them
within the boundaries of futility and finitude. Our happiness and the meaningfulness of our ordinary lives seem
slight in comparison with what's going down in the
world. But I am telling you: You are already utterly intimate with the power of this cosmos that beats your heart
and moves your breath and sex. You can enjoy this pure

intelligence, beauty and the function of Life's nurturing even in the midst of humanity's crippling difficulties.

The only way to limit our exposure to this pain and curb its emotional toll has seemed to be to withdraw from the human world to which we are yet necessarily connected through our work and social lives. It is not! We need involvement and community, relationship and love, but for many of us these beautiful expressions of Life exist in high tension and are dissipated through a sheer need to cope. The impossibility of physically taking ourselves out of the firing-range has instead meant a very troubling compromise: in order to remain involved, we have become desensitized. By this I mean something more than reaching a place of detachment in which we are unaffected by the trauma that surrounds us. What we are talking about is a literal desensitization: the shutting-down of our sensory awareness. This has only been added to by our subsuming in this impressive but soulless technological environment, which has effectively restructured our awareness in isolation from the Life-world, making us more responsive to the artificial beeps of our smartphones than to birdsong telling us of oncoming rain. When we consult the internet to be informed of the forecast instead of going outside to smell the air, feel humidity against our skin, perceive the quality of the light, and see the shape and speed of the clouds, we are simply not engaging the miraculous gifts of Life that are always available to us.

It's no wonder why we're miserable and strung-out. Intimacy can seem so foreign, so far removed from our own experiences. Although the reality of being alive means that we are constantly and fundamentally interconnected with the beauty and intelligence of Life itself, our sensory disengagement with others, the environment, and ourselves prevents us from really participating in our own lives with a profound depth of feeling. And when we are not participating fully in Life — body, breath, and sex — we are less than fully human. Instead of discovering ourselves in intimate contact and conviviality with the human and non-human world, we experience feelings of disconnection, isolation and loss. As we keep closing down, we lose sight of our absolute birthright: to give the truth of ourselves and be receptive of the caring wisdom of others and all that surrounds us. This is why we need the practical means of body and breath to recall our sensitivity and open our hearts to the awareness of Life's presence. By reclaiming our intimacy, every magnificence comes flooding through.

## Intimacy with Self

Just as intimacy begins in the heart, the experience of intimacy must begin with the most profoundly personal relationship we can ever know: Our relationship to our own selves. More than any other relationship in our lives, it is this innermost link to ourselves as Life that influences and shapes our experiences, colors our perception, and marks the place from which everything can either blossom abundantly or run astray. If we are the heartwood, this absolutely internal relationship is the nourishing condition that supports our growth and healing. It is intimacy with the self that is the basic foundation of honest and nurturing connections, whether with ourselves or with others. To the extent that our self-intimacy allows us to really own our expression of ourselves, through our inherently creative and unique ways of being, we light the way for all others in the world around us. But because intimacy is heartfelt, the cultivation of all intimacy must begin right here, at the heart: our being at home in the body and in the world.

When we speak of intimacy with the self, we are drawing upon the core understanding that our individual lives are nothing other than Life itself — literally. Every person is a unique expression of Life in both its seen and unseen dimensions. It is because of this that we are able to say that nothing is absent and there is no such thing as separation. There are no external goals or standards to be achieved as if we are not already full actualizations of the entire beauty, intelligence and wisdom of the universe. Everything it takes for this whole Reality to continue on its path of unfolding and reabsorbing — of releasing its strength into every birth, and receiving strength back in all passing — is fully present in us, as us, at all times. Life does not hold back. So every form, every manifestation, is fundamentally perfect as it is. The secrets of the universe are in us, as us.

Yet while intimacy is an idea promoted by culture, there are many limiting and uninspected cultural ideals about how we should relate to ourselves and others, and we have all been subjected to these constructs in one way or another. These can be as basic as our assumptions regarding the differences between how men and women should be or behave, or as complex as religious or philosophical traditions that treat human nature as a problem to be solved or overcome, or that heaven is a superior wonder to the Earth. Yet the one thing these cultural ideas all have in common is that they take us away from the actual, natural sense of simply being ourselves, which we are born with already in place. The looking for God assumes that God is absent, while the looking is itself the problem. Ideas that promote a sense of separation are cultural impositions restricting our natural state, and prevent us from feeling the truth of our absolute completeness. And like viruses they have invaded us. Their contagion resonates out from our relationship with self to penetrate and infect all of our relationships with others.

Intimacy is not only inevitable; it's already in place. It's fully active. All we're doing is making the enjoyment of it a practical part of our tool-kit for being alive in the world. Intimacy with yourself is the foundation on which to really honor your own story while expressing your culture, as all aspects of yourself, in individually creative and unique ways. With a little bit of practice — you might even think of it as housekeeping — the vibrancy of your naturally intimate condition will automatically come to shine forth in all of your relationships. You are a flower blooming in your own garden and the bees are buzzing. You don't need to grow in someone else's garden. There is no one remotely like you in the universe. You are a unique appearance of the power, beauty and intelligence of this cosmos.

Intimacy with the self is really an awareness of our natural state and our interrelatedness with all conditions and their perfection. But even more than that, it is something we instinctively feel in our bones and beneath our skin. Intimacy with self is an intuition and an orientation that cannot be put into words but pours forth from the depths of our understanding to be reflected in everything we do. Even our difficulties immediately and finally give us unique strengths and understanding. Those who have gone through their own suffering are the best teachers.

Yet although this intimacy is something that abides within us and wants for nothing more than exactly what we each already have — body, breath, and sex — the experience of it can be clouded over by the pressures of the external world and our indoctrinated tendency to conceptualize our bodies based on what they look like from the outside or in the mirror, and how media and social patterning suggest they should look like, rather than on how we are feeling inside. If we go on to construct value judgments about our social worth on these grounds of what we think we appear like to others, then instead of getting to know ourselves we get ensnared in ideas of how we could or should be. In short, our experiences become disconnected. Herein lies the grand illusion of separation. It's emotional quicksand, and it feels like crap. This is nothing other than a fragmentation of identity in which we treat the body as something extrinsically other than our true or highest or essential self or soul; and it is not natural — it has been put into us by culture, and it is the sticking-point when it comes to experiencing intimacy as our normal condition. At the same time, our desensitization, which we define as the shutting-off of our sensory and sensual awareness in order to withdraw from the pressures around us, makes us unaware of the constancy and stability that is ever-present within us.

This is the reason why intimacy starts with your own breath and body, with the healing of your own self. When we aren't feeling connected to our selves, most of us start mistaking other peoples' behavior and external events as somehow reflecting us. We end up falsely identifying with our responses to the unreliability that surrounds us; like hitting a beehive with a stick, our minds get shaken up and questions begin swarming that make us miserable. Over time, if we aren't receiving frequent enough reminders of how good and connected it is possible for us to feel; our negative feelings start solidifying a false self-identity. That swarm of questions may settle for short periods, but what about the next time, the following time, and the one after that? Our sense of self turns into a Pandora's box. We become afraid of our vulnerability and go to great lengths to protect our selves by forfeiting our softness. Instead of being open and welcoming, we put up hard walls between our selves, and others. And our misery just grows because we are too distrusting to reach out past our loneliness. We are no longer truly participating in our own lives. In other words, our intimacy — our deep sense of connectedness with our selves as unique and marvelous expressions of the Life force within — comes to be obscured with negativity. We even get attached to feeling bad because it seems more dependable than feeling good — and we tell ourselves that we're just being realistic. In the end, it often feels safer to just give in and accept that I'm not good enough or that I don't need anybody rather than go out on that limb of trust and confidence and get knocked back down again. These imaginary mental and emotional belief structures create physical illness, toxic chemistries and bio-imbalance in us. Our daily breathing practice restores intimacy and allows the body's healing chemistries to flourish. If we leave the body alone, relax in its inherent peace and Life's nurturing function then we are restored easily and naturally.

Intimacy is here, but if we aren't feeling it, it doesn't get incorporated into the way we see, experience, and express ourselves. The point is we go through an entire set of mental, emotional, and physical responses to what we think we've perceived. Although none of us are alone in our experiences of pain, this knowledge tends to reinforce negativity, rather than bringing us to, and enfolding us in, togetherness and solidarity. But the very same network of action and reaction that can get us down also serves our healing. We need to relearn our awareness of the roots of our existence; and this is achieved by tapping into those intimate structures of our being so that we recover the connectedness within. Hence the utter usefulness of actually bringing the movements of our body and breath together for a short time each day, to link the mind to its source, to the whole body of Life instead of sitting back and wishing for things to get better somehow. We stand up, center ourselves in our breath, introduce gentle movements, and find a much-needed sense of equilibrium that is ours and ours alone. The synchronization of these movements effectively heals our desensitization, allowing us to undergo an expansion of awareness through which we once again become aware of the beating of our hearts.

As the mind is allowed to settle, we redevelop consciousness of our inner connectedness. We lift the veil off our participation in our own lives. We can feel the sounds of Life within us; and it makes us receptive to Life all around us. We see the upheavals on the surface as just that, superficial, and relax instead into direct understanding that in the depths of our waters is absolute calm.

The observation of our disturbance is the unavoidable motive of practice. So we can even be grateful for the pain. It moves us to do something practical about it. Nonetheless, while the practice of body and breath is incredibly simple, and the reclaiming of our selves through intimacy is powerfully healing and leads to an abiding awareness of Life within, sometimes we encounter stumbling blocks. You see, whether we begin our practice out of curiosity and experimentation, or whether we begin it with an already-established knowledge of the fact that we need daily practice to see real transforming changes, there comes a point for most of us when we have to let go of what we think we know. We must leave everything we know behind. This typically means releasing our strong-hold on the ideas that make us think we are secure but are actually social restrictions imposed on the unfolding of our self-awareness and identity-in-intimacy. When we are so accustomed to resorting to strength in our need to cope, it takes courage and trust — in others, but in ourselves foremost — to learn to soften like this.

Like our tree with its strong trunk, we need the soft foliage above to receive the nutrients that feed our strength. For some, it quickly comes as an immense sense of relief to find that we are more than okay just as we are; for others, the relief comes gradually as they step for the first time into a vast and unknown landscape in which there are no standards to be met. It can even feel like we're losing a grip on ourselves as we lose the familiar, if unloved boundaries that we all come to rely upon for structure in our self-identity — but there is no loss of identity here, just an exquisite magnification of self in its absolute intimacy with Life. Our strength begins to receive as we drink in the nutrients of life, thirsty from the desert. It makes our strength stronger, more durable and intelligent. You cannot lose yourself or find yourself because you already are your self. For everyone it is usually a gradual process with perhaps sudden blinding breakthroughs in the simple realization that we are perfect as Life itself.

Finally, it is true that there are times for all of us when it is completely daunting to realize that there is nothing outside of the present moment, that everything we need is right here now, and that there is no way out, that there is no reason to find a way out. This is because as our intimacy with self quickens, revealing its inherent momentum and force, our only option is an honesty so richly warm and loving that it pulls us right out of the deep-freeze of denial. Our past can confront and startle us as we start to see the traumas inflicted on us, and the realization of the lengths we go to not to feel them. Yet it is at this very second, too, that some certain and very natural understandings unfurl: there is no truth outside of our awareness, because our bodies and minds are utterly open and unlimited. There is no need to look further. The deepest mystery and greatest love of the universe unfolds in every breath we take — and it reveals nothing other than ourselves.

## Intimacy with Each Other in the World

When we let go of culturally endorsed spiritual goals and unnecessary thought-patterns to allow Life to flow vitally throughout our entire selves, there inevitably occurs an expansion of feeling outwards from the heart. Our behavior and relationships start attuning naturally with the intimacy that has become the baseline of our lived-awareness, our emotions and actions. The synchronization of body and breath is crucially linked with this development, for it is a practical and actual means to reclaiming personal awareness of our inner stability and the union of opposites by which the source of opposites, the heart, is realized. The heart is felt as the depthless root of all perceptions, all relationship. The deep-seated sense of equilibrium that arises through daily practice not only cultivates the real feeling of our own internal-external connectedness, but also reopens the doors of our sensory perception in such a way that we are able to see that all others are suffused with the same intensities of Life, light and consciousness as we are. We really know that we are connected with all of Life because we really can feel it. And just as our beautifully intimate heart-identity is made real to us, we share this reality or live it out through our relationships with the world outside our body. There is a profound movement of feeling from within the depths of the heart to without, and back again.

Ultimately, our total connectedness is shared with all human and non-human others as we relearn ourselves though intimate relationship with Life itself and grow open to the extraordinary wonder of our ordinary condition. We find that we have no argument with what is. No argument with the ocean, only embrace. No argument with the sun, only gratitude. No argument with the animal kingdom, only love. No argument with the plant kingdom, only symbiotic nurturing and healing relationship. But when it comes to humans? Oh well, that's another story! However, recognition of the beauty of all in the one reality we all share leads us to embrace the human domain with grace and gratitude, too. We are no longer in conflict with society even as it struggles on. We teach and contribute something positive to this suffering world.

It is important to be mindful that when we speak of human relationship here, we're referring to all of our interactions with everything and everyone, both romantic and not, but not in the taken-for-granted sense of "relationship" that our society typically presumes. Simply being related to someone by blood or friendship or marriage does not sufficiently account for the depths of sublime relationship that is our birthright. We have this conventional idea of what a relationship means, and it tends to be built up around expectations and obligations regarding what we think we should be getting and giving. But it's clear that this "like it or not" attitude just isn't working for the majority of us, for if it did, all those relationship gurus would be out of a job. It's possible for our parents to commit their energy to raising us, but that doesn't automatically mean that we feel loved, supported, or understood. It's possible for our partners to do their fair share of work around the house, spend time with us and offer practical support, but again that doesn't always mean that we don't feel frustrated, claustrophobic, unsatisfied or lonely. In fact, there probably have been times when we've all experienced situations like this — and, moreover, times when we ourselves have been accused of apathy. It is really a basic mistake, to confuse doing our duty with real embrace, real delight and real care in relationship. The difference between the two is simple, like the difference between your partner cooking every second night because that's the deal and them noticing that you aren't feeling well and respond-ing with insight and tenderness. The first scenario could be acted-out by a robot; the second requires intimacy and its awareness.

What most of us are missing in our relationships is the sincere honesty of intimacy, a depth of feeling. So, while we may be living in the same space, what we aren't necessarily doing is relating — we talk without commu-nicating, listen without hearing. What we need to do is redefine relationship in light of our living, breathing intimacy with all conditions of Life. And when we do this, what we find is that a relationship is a quality of presence. Relationships describe our participation in our own lives. The integrity of relationship is something that blossoms through the profound feeling that arises when we are able to be really present and aware of the com-mon intimacy that circulates and connects us with every other person and thing around us.

There are very many reasons for a lack of feeling in relationship. Every single reason involves an absence of self-intimacy, colored further by previous traumas in the usual life that society presents. It is hurtful and confus-ing to discover that what we've been shown of relation-ships — from our earliest experiences of our parents' interaction to depictions in the media and what we hear from friends — just doesn't serve us. Our feelings of reluctance and uncertainty are certainly justified in so many respects, but none of them change the fact that this slithering sense of isolation is just not appropriate to the truth of Life.

The point is, we don't have to stumble blind in the dark. There is a way and a means in everyone's reach, and it starts with the breath. It is fearless, generous, soft and strong, strength receiving as we commit the inhalation to the exhalation. It is literally the merging of the male and female aspects of your own embodiment. It is making love with Life. These very qualities reflect Life's presence within us, allowing us to extend forward from the heart and relate with each other in a way that is absolutely authentic. Genuine relationships take the willingness to stick it through, to support and protectively nurture each other's healing, and ultimately to move forward hand-in-hand. This is especially the case in our romantic relationships, where we tend to have so much on the line (or fight so hard to keep our vulnerabilities off the line) and so much sexual dysfunction to heal that when things get rough it's not uncommon to respond with a flight or fight reaction. If we're going to be honest about these things, then we have to admit that our current society doesn't present us with solid models of healthy relationships.

We are surrounded with the tattered remains of angry stories, bitterness, and disappointment. To sit in the middle of so many tensions — and we all find ourselves here at some point — can suffocate and disorient our natural and trusting expression of ourselves; and even if we personally have managed to hold on to a sense of open-heartedness, chances are that we still encounter potential partners who carry a backlog of sorrowful experiences that become restrictions to our own openness.

Once again, this is where self-intimacy comes to the rescue. Rejection and avoidance of intimacy — sometimes termed as "independence" — does nothing but fence us off from our fullest expression of self. Autonomy, on the other hand, is something expansive that is only truly discovered in the context of relationship.

By acknowledging and then forgiving your own history of limitation and pain, that pain is released and the space opens for connection to come flooding through. Cultivate your own intimacy with all of Life, and gift it to those around you. Let all your traumatized personas of the past know that you — the adult survivor — have survived and that you are alive and well. Comfort all of them and let them know they did a good job in the circumstance. They got you to where you are today. Honor their pain, and your present pain. It is the healing function of nurturing Life. Make friends and embrace all your stages in your life's timeline, in the one celebration of your entire life so far. Stand in your own beautiful ground. In intimate partnership you are healing the entire human dysfunction of male-female polarity. You have the tools and the insight now. You will do it for yourself, your ancestors and all future generations.

With time, the inner awareness of connectedness will bring about a reevaluation of habits and relationships. This often happens when we embark on our journey of self-healing and nurturing; and while it is utterly appropriate and is nothing more than the process of dissolving those fears and feelings that no longer serve us, these waters can be muddy. Sometimes, when we start feeling more connected to ourselves, we can start feeling less connected with those people around us — including especially our partners — who we imagine are not participating in a similar path of growth. Instead of feeling intimate with them, we get judgmental because we perceive a reluctance to heal. This can fuel angst, a sense of suspicion that our partner's approach to life is either going to hold us back or indicates a lack of investment in understanding us; however, this may not be the case, and it is important to keep re-grounding in the rich depths of our own intimate connectedness when such feelings arise.

Once we have experienced a glimmering sense of the peaceful vitality within us, and had a taste of its promise for our being-in-the-world, it is very easy to get caught up in the dream and glitter of our "higher self." And from there, it is even easier to either reject partnering altogether ("I don't need this") or seek obsessively for a partner who you perceive as an equal on the path. But this is not the way. To go sifting through partners like seeking a flawless diamond among the sediment of costume jewels is not the approach. It serves no one, and is an inherent denial of Life's perfection. Know that every person is already a diamond, just as you are. Know that every person has been wounded by the bloodstained violent history of humankind, just as you have. It is imperative that we work together, rather than perpetuating the cycle and self-fulfilling prophecy of disappointment. Sometimes we do have to hold the fort for one another, to give each other the space to uncover our own stories and recognize our selves. There are statements from the great traditions that say, "Love fails not when you are unloved but when you fail to love", or "turn the other cheek". Then we do not crush the flowing petals of our own heart. This healing is central to an authentically intimate relationship. We are all healing in our own unique ways and time. Love is hard work done easily.

As we have said the self is ultimately realized only in the related condition of all Life. There IS no separate capsule of energy that is you, seductive as that may be. Yet all our spiritual models, heroes, saints and sages are generally women-less men (or vice versa) teaching ideas of self-sufficiency. Imagine if Christ, the Buddha, Mohammed and the Popes had wives of equal social status and visibility. What sort of culture would have been created? The paradox is that many such saints actually were in partnership, though it was kept hidden from or by orthodoxy. This fault of civilization is something we can now correct in the understanding that there is no male without female, no inner without outer, etc. And participation in the opposites is the very spiritual process, which reveals the truth we seek. When we participate and understand ourselves to be involved in all of Life's conditions, the quality of our presence to one another is heightened; our self-acceptance blooms in forgiveness, patience and empathic receptivity of the world.

∞

Email to Mark Whitwell
Name: Nicki Kreutzer
Subject: Thank you

Dear Mark,

Led by extraordinary circumstances I had come to join the Moksha LA Yoga festival in July 2015. I ended up, jetlagged, taking only one class: yours. I had no idea who you were. So I sat there open minded, tired. You just said to a friend "everyone that needs to be here is here, so close the door" — and all of a sudden I was wide awake. I probably didn't look awake and there was no physical reason to be, :) but be sure, I was.

The things you have said that hour about the breath enveloping the movement in the polarity of above to below, strength receiving, the male/female union, within and without, and us as individuals being the proof of the power of this universe, this unbelievable body, asking us to promise to do the suggested sun salutation in a relaxed way, keeping the focus on the breath, they have stuck with me deeply. At the end you said to your friend: "They promised to do it 40 days. We have accomplished much today."

You know how it sometimes works, you hear something, and a sentence can change your entire life. Well, it stuck with me more than I would have expected as if it changed some wires in my head or something, back to the right place. As I could not forget what you had said, I got interested in what else you might say and got your book Yoga of Heart and read it these past couple of weeks.

Today I watched a video on YouTube of you giving a class, "The Promise of Healing Connection", and this finally did it. I gotta write you.

Dear Mark, thank you so much for taking the time and effort to talk about reality the way you do.

Your words have resonated with me from the first time I met you and I know they are true. I know it from my own experience, in contrast from the way I feel when I read something that I haven't experienced yet. As you pointed out: You have an experience and if you then read the ancient texts, you recognize their truth inside. You know from your own experience that they are true.

I understand the difficulty to reach people that haven't woken up yet. But I believe even if they might not yet understand what we are talking about at the moment, it happens; something inside of them hears the truth and "moves"... like a flame that moves all of a sudden with a little breeze. They might not recognize it right away, but will, and others will feel the same way. Or perhaps never, being seriously distracted. It doesn't matter. But I was very happy to hear and recognize the truth — much like coming home.

So thank you for reminding us of home and reminding us that others know too where it is and love home as much as we do.

I am becoming a teacher and sometimes feel frustrated already. The expectation of what a yoga class is about (fitness for example) and my understanding of yoga. It seems difficult to pick people up to find common ground to stand on and do something together. It's fun watching you do it.

Your friend,

Nicki
Dusseldorf, Germany

# Physical Intimacy

Although intimacy has every relevance to how we do our sexual loving, popular conceptions of intimacy as sex are reductive and don't even come close to the vastness of this wonder. Intimacy is physical. It is a physical truth. This is an inescapable reality, because as we have seen, intimacy is a description of your entire being — of how the worlds inside and outside of your body are continually married in your awareness. Sex is not intimacy, yet it is a means of sharing and communicating profound intimacy. Intimacy is entirely expressed by all sensory function, including sex.

The problem lies with our social attitudes to sex, or, more specifically, our dysfunctional communication about it. The generations of religious denial of sex has created the vast exaggeration of sex, the burden of pornography. In religious institutions and in society itself sex bursts out as illness, abuse and life-denying negativity. In life we oscillate between celibacy and the exaggeration of sex, and neither work. Because we are still awkward in communicating openly and naturally about our physical needs for closeness and sexual fulfillment, we carry on as though we were divorced from our innate sexuality. We either repress ourselves with a sense of awkwardness and shame or objectify and exaggerate ourselves with socially contrived sexiness in a way that belittles our true depth of feeling. Both responses are reactive — an avoidance of the feelings of open vulnerability that arise from intimacy with another. Not only do we lack a wholesome education in these matters but also when we are uncomfortable with our own bodies it is impossible to be comfortable with another's. We all need sex, just as Life needs sex for regeneration, nurturing and survival! Yet we want to run away from what we might reveal in our physical and emotional nudity. This isn't just about hiding it away from others — it's about hiding it from our selves too. Let's be honest: sex can be scary. Until we have a way of negotiating this terrain with peace and acceptance, for so long as sex is separated from intimacy, our dissatisfaction simply continues.

It's time to set some facts straight. We've already discovered that the full force of Life exists within us; we are not separate from Life itself. Life's natural course and only interest lies in continuity and evolution of Life. And how does that continuation take place? In the meeting of all opposites, masculine and feminine, inside and out, body, breath and mind. Sex is a pure expression of this meeting, an upsurge of Life's intimacy throughout our own bodies to encapsulate and entwine with the life force flowing through another. That's how powerful sex is. It cannot be denied; but we have been caught up in a cultural madness that has tried to do just this. Sex is a loving extension from the heart, the place where all Life starts. In the face of such great wonder, there is no room for shame. Forgive yourself and everyone else now and let it all go. You are perfect as you are. In fact, you couldn't be better.

Because of the mess that surrounds sex, this opening of awareness takes time and discipline. For some of us, this means actually engaging our selves or our partner sexually when we might have fallen out of that saddle. For others of us, it means recalibrating our approach to sex, learning to give and receive with openhanded, openhearted sincerity instead of masking our selves beneath layers of shameful or exaggerated behaviors. It is only by coming together, by practicing our loving in total honesty, that sex expands as regeneration, realization, and healing. And when anxiousness, sorrow, and other feelings come up that stand between you and your awareness of the complete perfection within, just breathe through them and let them pass. In the context of loving relationship, all sorts of flotsam come to the surface. Wave it goodbye — it's just your soul letting go of obstructions it doesn't need anymore. Hold onto the stuff that isn't holding you back. Remember: "Love brings up everything that is un-love so that it may be seen and understood."

There is, of course, the situation where no amount of loving undoes the knot of belief patterns between two people, and there is no choice but to separate and try again with someone else. But this cannot be done casually. We can only leave when there is truly no ambiguity. After a long and sincere time of testing your love, it may simply become clear that you are not suited as intimate partners due to complex patterns that the relationship does not heal despite the good-will to try and work things out over a sustained time. Then make your separation as dignified and gracious as your sacred coming together. Be grateful for all that the relationship has done for you both, all that it has healed. Try to forgive and do not leave with bitterness that must be healed later.

No one can do it for you. Make an appointment with yourself to do your Promise breathing practice every day. Make appointments to make love with your intimate other with a frequency that you both agree upon. Do this in the context of every other kind of intimate activity that you enjoy together. By establishing strength and receptivity in our own embodiment first, we are then able to practice exactly that with our partner. In physical loving the bodies know what to do in sensitive regard for each other, perfectly giving while perfectly receiving. There is no performance required, no manual required, nothing to worry about. Just do your yoga. Do your Life. Do your loving. When we feel slighted or hurt by another's fear or failure, just continue to do your loving. Remember! Love fails not when we are unloved, but when we fail to love.

We discover for ourselves that there is nothing stronger than the softness of allowing ourselves to be vulnerable and open. There is nothing meek about love; nothing subordinate about heartfelt care. When we extend out from the connectedness within, we cultivate a maturity of surrender so great that only love is strong enough to bear it. Inhale, and receive the tender grace of Life's utterly confident strength all around you. Exhale, and return your strength through infinite receptivity to the needs of every other. Our heartbeat, breath, and sex are the purest expression of Life's self-awareness within the inner structures of our being.

My teachers taught me The Promise Practice. I teach you exactly as they taught me. It is wisdom's nurturing force, flowing from ancient times to now. I give it to you so you can practice and pass it forward. Please teach your friends and families. Intimacy with body, breath and relationships is everyOne's birthright. This can now spread at a grass roots level as the unifying principle of all cultures and all people in the one intimacy with breath and the Life we all share. By enjoying your Life you will spread intimacy in the world. This is how it will grow. You do not need to burn yourself out in this mission. The flower does not advertise its own fragrance yet its effects are profound, flower to flower, and person to person. Wherever The Promise is taught, intimate groups of friends are formed who practice together and care for each other. I have seen this happen all around the world and it gives us the intimate community we all long for, even in the midst of difficulty. I experienced Arab and Jewish practitioners reaching out with deep concern for each other during a dreadful war between their nations. The one Life we share was obviously more the point to them than religious difference or boundaries. They are able to celebrate the awesome differences between cultures. They are not in fear of an "other."

If you are already participating in intimate traditions such as Buddhism, Christianity, Hinduism, Islam, Judaism, agnosticism, atheism or any derivative thereof, traditional or new age, please teach The Promise Practice in that context. It will add an enriching intimacy to your community and is the practical means by which the ideals of faith based systems are realized and enjoyed. Without these practical tools of real intimate connection, the sublime expressions of text have made matters worse for humanity due to the stark and painful difference between bland daily social patterns and those wonderful ideas that are far removed from actual experience. The Promise, practiced daily, actually and naturally and non-obsessively, will heal this imagined divide between matter and spirit. Peace is breaking out all around and together we will educate and heal the world with this soothing balm. This is the hope for humanity.

In ancient times, the frequency of individuals passing into perfect freedom was very rare. So rare, that such activity in society created upheaval, even revolution and ongoing political religious histories. Appearances by beings such as Jesus or Gautama were so stunning that major world empires organized around them, creating a phenomenal spread of doctrine through out lands. In contemporary times, however, such freedom is in the domain of ordinary people and the frequency of such people appearing is now more common. Indeed, it has been predicted in the great tradition that realization would be on a mass scale, very attainable and obvious to the broad public. This is the time we live in of mass communication and travel. We are ordinary humans, ordinary Buddhas, and freedom is occurring in ordinary life without fanfare or exaggeration. You will simply be surprised when you find yourself to be in perfect peace and perfect intimacy with all that is. This is now our human possibility.

Remember, your body is naturally a peaceful organism. Life is nurturing you and you cannot come to any harm in this universe. You are in safe hands. Yet humanity has been burdened by culture and that has, in most cases, been detrimental until real intimacy can be established within them. These days, in the wholesale homogenization of world cultures, where no one lives the life of their parents, no one knows anything for certain and instability is all around, yet it is a time of great spiritual opportunity. All this froth and foam is because we are in shallow waters, so someone like you, with little training, can find yourself on dry land. I believe someone like you can bring others to the shore. Please make that your goal.

## Exercise Four: Putting It All Together

On the following pages you'll find a simple sequence of yoga postures that you can practice together or individually. Apply the techniques you've learned so far; breathing with sound and enveloping each movement with the breath. Repeat each movement, called 'vinyasa', a few times before moving on.

## 01. INHALATION, EXHALATION

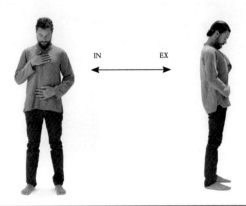

Stand with your feet hip width and parallel. Place one hand on your upper chest and one hand on your lower belly. As you inhale through your nose, feel the hand above lift as your chest expands. As you exhale out your nose, draw in your abdominals, gently pushing the air out.

## 02. BREATHING WITH THE ARMS

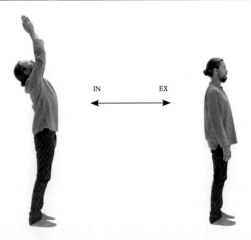

Stand with your feet hip width and parallel. Begin with your arms relaxed at your sides. Exhale completely. Inhale and raise your arms overhead, lifting your head to see your hands come together. Exhale and lower your arms.

## 03. FORWARD BEND

IN      EX

*Inhale and raise your arms overhead as before. Exhale and bend forward at the waist keeping your knees soft. At the end of the exhale your head should be completely relaxed and knees bent. Inhale and return to standing with arms overhead, moving them in a circle around your body.*

## 04. STRIDING FORWARD BEND

IN      EX

*From standing, stride one leg back a comfortable distance keeping feet hip width. Inhale and raise your arms overhead, lifting your head to see your hands come together. Exhale and bend forward, bringing your hands to the floor.*

## 05. FORWARD BEND WITH TWIST

*Stand with your feet wider than your shoulders. Inhale and lift your arms parallel to the floor, keeping your chin down. Exhale and bend forward with arms extended, twisting toward your right foot. Look up toward your top hand. Inhale and return to the starting position, alternating sides each exhalation.*

## 06. CAT ARCH, CHILD POSE

*Begin on your hands and knees. Inhale as you lift your head and chest. Exhale and come into a deep crouch, hips towards your heels.*

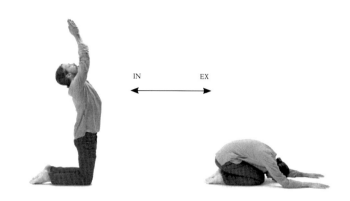

IN          EX

Starting from Child Pose, inhale as you stand on your knees sweeping your arms overhead. Look up to see your palms come together. Exhale and return to the starting position, keeping your arms stretched out in front or bringing them to your low back.

IN          EX

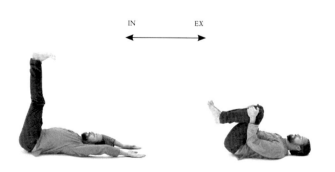

Begin on your back with your knees toward your chest. Inhale and straighten your legs toward the roof, bringing your arms straight overhead. Exhale, drawing your abdominals in as your knees come toward your chest.

## 09. BRIDGE

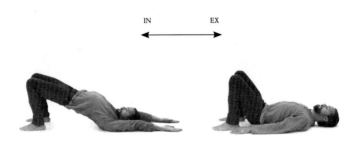

On your back, bring your feet to the floor keeping them about hip width, arms resting at your side. Inhale and press through your feet to raise your hips, bringing your arms straight up overhead. Exhale as you lower your hips and arms.

## 10. RESTORATIVE

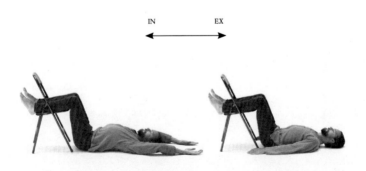

Rest your legs on a chair or sofa, arms at your side. Inhale and slowly bring your arms overhead, backs of your hands to the floor. Exhale and slowly return your arms to your side. An option would be to raise one arms at a time.

Surrender, known in the traditions as
*Isvarapranidhana*, and faith, known as *sraddha*,
is the giving up of spiritual ideas.

It is simply clear that the wonder of Life and its
source is our natural condition and already utterly
established in us as us. this is perfect faith in, and
surrender to, Life; whatever Life is altogether in its
extreme intelligence and vast interrelatedness.

Actual yoga then arises naturally as the
movement of Life in body, breath and relationship
rather than the manipulation of Life and the qualifying
of the living organism with concepts and effort in
mind and body.

You are the power of the cosmos arising as
pure intelligence, beauty and function.
There is only reality.
Nothing else.

— *From the Hridayasutra, Mark Whitwell*

*Lie down on your back and let the body release and relax, completely supported by
the ground. Keep your legs open and allow your feet to fall gently to the sides. Rest
your arms at your side with your palms turned up. Let your breathing return to it's
natural rhythm and allow your mind to rest in your whole body.*

# THERE IS NO MANUAL REQUIRED, NOTHING TO WORRY ABOUT.

# JUST DO YOUR YOGA. DO YOUR LIFE. DO YOUR LOVING.

## About the Author

Mark Whitwell is interested in developing an authentic yoga practice for the individual, based on the teachings of T. Krishnamacharya and his son TKV Desikachar, with whom he enjoyed a relationship for more than twenty years. Mark's teachings clarify the profound passion and relevance of ancient wisdom to contemporary life.

For the past twenty-five years, Mark has travelled the globe teaching yoga to thousands of people. He was the editor and contributor to TKV Desikachar's book *The Heart of Yoga*, and is the author of *The Yoga of Heart* and *The Promise of Love, Sex and Intimacy.*

For more information and events, visit *www.heartofyoga.org*

Download the iPromise app on iTunes and Google Play

49989898R00062

Made in the USA
Middletown, DE
25 October 2017